Blackpool Trams & Recollections 19

Barry McLoughlin

Contents

Silver Link Publishing Ltd
The Trundle
Ringstead Road
Great Addington
Kettering
Northants NN14 4BW

Tel/Fax: 01536 330588

email: sales@nostalgiacollection.com
Website: www.nostalgiacollection.com

Acknowledgements

Many sources were used in the production of this book, but particularly valuable were Steve Palmer's series of erudite volumes on the Blackpool tramway; *Blackpool Tramways 1933-66* by Stephen Lockwood (Middleton Press); *The Blackpool Tramway* (The Tramway Museum Society); the ever-informative and sometimes trenchant *Trams Magazine;* and the websites of the Blackpool Heritage Trust: *www.blackpoolheritage.com/htrust/* and British Trams Online: *www.britishtramsonline.co.uk.*

But the most heartfelt thanks must go to the late Ray Ruffell, who had the foresight to take these wonderfully evocative pictures at a time when the future of the tramway was by no means secure.

All the images in this book are from the Ray Ruffell collection, which is held by the publisher. Ray was a railwayman, transport enthusiast and photographer of equal merit who travelled all over the country in pursuit of his hobby and his art.

Dedication

To Hannah and Alex

First published in 2016

British Library Cataloguing in Publication Data
A catalogue record for this book is available from the British Library.

Printed and bound in the Czech Republic

About the author

Barry McLoughlin is the author of eight books on the railways and tramways of Blackpool and the Fylde.

A former editor of *Steam World*, Britain's biggest-selling historical railway magazine, he spent ten years as sub-editor of *RAIL* and *Steam Railway* magazines, to which he still contributes.

A journalist for more than 40 years, he started his career on the *Warrington Guardian*. For 15 years he worked on the *Blackpool Gazette*, including a spell as its parliamentary correspondent at Westminster, and is now a freelance writer and editor for a variety of publications.

Title page: **TOWER** Four Blackpool landmarks on 24 July (from right) are: the Woolworth's building, the Tower, Lewis's and, on the corner of Church Street, the former Burton's Tailors. Only the Tower retains its original function today. The trams are OMO car No 3 and twin-cars 677/687.

STARR GATE Pioneer one-man operated (OMO) car No 1 leaves Starr Gate for Little Bispham on 28 July past the car park that today is the location of the new £20 million tramway depot. Behind the tram's trolley tower is the welcome arch for the Illuminations. Beyond and to the right of the tram is the popular Lemon Tree nightclub, now replaced by flats, and Pontin's Holiday Centre, opposite the sandhills, which closed in 2009 after nearly 50 years and has now been demolished to make way for housing.

NEW SOUTH PROMENADE In 1926 Lord Derby opened New South Promenade from the Pleasure Beach to Starr Gate, with a tramway extension along its entire length, which brought the Blackpool network to its fullest extent. (Closures started barely ten tears later.) The new promenade was the site of some of Blackpool's smartest hotels but today is sadly in decline, with several of them boarded up. On 28 July, Balloons 719 (leading) and 710 approach the terminus at Starr Gate. Car 719, dating from 1935, has been adapted as part of Blackpool's 'B' Fleet of modified Balloon trams.

PLEASURE BEACH The turning circle at the Pleasure Beach, which was introduced in 1937, was a popular place for enthusiasts to see a bevy of Balloon trams. On 30 July, 712 prepares for its short trip to the Tower, while 701 and 718, plus one other double-decker and an open Boat, wait in the background.

PLEASURE BEACH OMO car No 3 nears the end of its journey to the Pleasure Beach and will soon be heading back north via the turning circle on 28 July. On the right is the entrance to the Pleasure Beach's Casino building, a striking piece of 1930s Art Deco by the celebrated modernist architect Joseph Emberton.

Left: **PLEASURE BEACH** An inspector supervises the busy high-summer tram traffic at the Pleasure Beach on 28 July, with double-decker 726 leading the line-up.

Right: **PLEASURE BEACH** Open Boat car 603, built by English Electric in 1934, waits on the turning circle at the Pleasure Beach on 28 July. Like its sister 605, it is now preserved in the United States.

LYTHAM ROAD Progress twin-set 671 (towing car) and 681 (trailer) head from the depot along a visitor-packed Lytham Road to Manchester Square and the promenade on 3 August. The 'Nip-In' Café is advertising on its blackboard: Tea, Ground Coffee, Horlicks, Bovril and Milk Shakes to 'eat in' or 'take away'.

Photo	DESTINATIONS
9	TOWER
10	TOWER
11	TOWER
12	TOWER
13	TOWER
14	TOWER
15	TOWER

TOWER Overshadowed by the distinctive honeycombed frontage of Lewis's department store, OMO No 6 and Balloon 715 pick up passengers at the Tower on 22 July. The double-decker is now part of the Heritage Fleet. The ultra-modern outlines of the Lewis's building were a Golden Mile landmark for 30 years from 1964. It had itself replaced another emblematic Blackpool building, the Palace Theatre (formerly the Alhambra), which closed in 1961.

Above: **TOWER** Illuminated frigate 736 *HMS Blackpool* navigates past the three-track layout at the Tower on 29 July. Rebuilt from Pantograph car 170 in 1965, it was withdrawn in 2001 but returned for the 2004 Lights and is still operational as part of the Heritage Fleet following refurbishment.

Left: **TOWER** A wonderful shot by Ray Ruffell of English Electric double-decker 701 passing Lewis's department store en route to Fleetwood on 24 July, with the Tower in the background. The Balloon car, dating from 1934, is today preserved in striking red and white livery as part of the Heritage Fleet. In 2014 it was restored to its 1991 condition with financial support from Fylde Tramway Society.

Left: **TOWER** The beautiful 1890s red brickwork of the Grade 1 listed Tower building forms the backdrop on 22 July for OMO car No 3, converted in 1972 from English Electric railcoach 610.

Right: **TOWER** Introduced in 1934, the open Boats were, and still are, ever-popular with holidaymakers. Boat 603 runs between the Tower and North Pier on 25 July. The Burton's building is occupied by the fashion store Diana Warren, which sold stylish day and evening wear for women.

TOWER The turret of the Palatine Hotel on the extreme right of this picture is another promenade landmark that is long gone. Another, though much less-missed, feature is the awning outside the Tower entrance, which has now been removed to reveal the original brickwork and stained glass beneath. Brush railcoach 635 heads to Fleetwood on 22 July.

TOWER The five floors of Lewis's helped make Blackpool one of the shopping capitals of the North West, with no fewer than three big department stores. All are now gone, and Blackpool was left without a single department store until the opening in 2008 of the new Debenham's in the Hounds Hill Centre. On 22 July, twin-car set 687/677 passes on its way to the Pleasure Beach.

North Pier

NORTH PIER One-man operated cars No 3 (leading) and No 4 head towards the Pleasure Beach at Talbot Square on 25 July. An application for a Transport and Works Act Order (TWA) to extend the tramway from Talbot Square to North Station was made by Blackpool Council in July 2016. If it is approved, construction should begin in early 2018 and services could start the following April. A further two Bombardier Flexity 2 trams have been ordered to work the additional services. The double-track route would allow direct tram services to run once more from North Station to the south and north of the town. The tramway along Talbot Road to Layton was the first to be abandoned, in 1936, together with the Central Drive route.

NORTH PIER Photographer Ray Ruffell's wife and daughter, Joan and Margaret, wait to cross the tram tracks at North Pier on 27 July as Balloon 706 heads for Uncle Tom's Cabin.

NORTH PIER Car 600 was the pioneer Boat tram and is still operating. Sponsored by Fylde Tramway Society, it was named *Duchess of Cornwall* in 2007, and the Prince of Wales's wife travelled on it during a visit to Blackpool the following year. On 25 July 1973 it has a full complement of passengers, two of whom wave to the photographer, near North Pier.

Right: **NORTH PIER** A busy scene at Talbot Square on 25 July. The fashions of the 1970s are much in evidence as the two conductors on Balloon 702 enjoy a break, about to be joined by the driver. Behind Bispham-bound Boat 603 is Butlin's Hotel, with the War Memorial on the left.

Left: **NORTH PIER** Two members of the 1930s Streamliner family of trams introduced by Walter Luff stand at North Pier on 27 July: Brush railcoach 625 and an unidentified Balloon double-decker.

1973 Blackpool Happenings

Edward Heath addresses his last party conference as Prime Minister at the Winter Gardens

Love Thy Neighbour is staged at the Winter Gardens Theatre

Freddie Starr appears in *Showtime '73* at the North Pier Theatre

Mike Yarwood and Basil Brush headline in *Holiday Startime* at the ABC Theatre

Danny La Rue stars in *International Spectacular '73* at the Opera House

The Dixieland Palace and Golden Goose entertainment complex at the shore end of Central Pier is gutted by fire but later rebuilt

Blackpool Tower and its buildings are designated as Grade 1 listed

The Winter Gardens complex is designated a Grade 2* listed building

The Tower's menagerie closes after the opening of Blackpool Zoo the previous year

Blackpool FC finish seventh in Division Two. In their third and final appearance in the Anglo-Italian Cup, the former winners are knocked out in the fourth round

Former England goalkeeper Gordon Banks switches on the Illuminations

Bob and Terry enjoy an outing to Blackpool in *Whatever Happened to the Likely Lads?*

Wendy Anne George wins the Miss Blackpool title

NORTH PIER With the Midland Bank, now the Counting House, in Talbot Square on the right, 1953 Coronation car 662 heads off to complete its journey to Starr Gate on 28 July. The building to the rear of the tram on the corner of Queen's Square, housing the long-established Town and Country Restaurant, is now the successful Soul Suite, which has been playing soul and Motown music since 2005.

NORTH PIER Milady sweets, produced by a well-known Blackpool confectionery firm, were a big advertiser on the town's trams. At Talbot Square on 25 July, Balloons 721 (leading) and 713 both carry its advertising. Behind them is single-deck railcoach 625.

NORTH PIER Passengers queue to board OMO car No 7, which was converted from railcoach 619, at North Pier on 24 July. In the background are two of Blackpool's grandest hotels, the Metropole (left) and the Clifton (behind the tram).

NORTH PIER This time advertising Milady Treacle Toffee, Balloon double-decker 715 passes Talbot Square en route to the Pleasure Beach on 25 July. Passing the tram is a Morris Oxford and behind that about to turn right is a relatively rare Lancia Fulvia. Disappearing to the left behind the tram is an Austin 1800.

NORTH PIER The twin-car sets, converted from railcoaches in the late 1950s and early 1960s, with newly built trailers, were a big hit both with the public and the tramway operator as they provided comfort and high capacity at relatively low cost, although they did require two conductors. On 31 July, motor car 671 provides the power behind trailer 681 at Talbot Square heading to Bispham. Car 671 survives as part of the Blackpool Heritage Trust collection, though its trailer is preserved elsewhere.

NORTH PIER Freddie Starr is still starring in *Showtime '73* at the North Pier Theatre on 31 July while Coronation 655 picks up passengers for its journey to Fleetwood. Introduced in Coronation year, 1953, the elegant, 8ft-wide trams seated 56, but operational problems belied their handsome exteriors.

NORTH PIER An imposing array of trams including, (left to right), Nos 618, 672/682 and 634 at North Pier on 27 July, though the wear and tear on the track surface because of the volume of traffic is apparent. No 634 was privately purchased following withdrawal in 2007 and having spent some time undergoing restoration, by the owner and his daughter, at the Rushden Historical Transport Society in Northamptonshire, it was moved and spent two years at the North East Land Sea and Air Museum at Washington near Sunderland. No 634 returned to Blackpool on 28 February 2016 having been generously donated to the Blackpool Heritage Trust.

Left: **NORTH PIER** Occasionally a power failure could produce a 'tram jam' like this one at North Pier on 27 July. Progress twin-car 676/686 is among trams waiting patiently to continue.

Right: **NORTH PIER** Blackpool Zoo had opened the previous year and the banner across the promenade road encourages tourists to visit on the No 21 bus, as twin-car set 675/685 passes on its way from North Pier on 24 July. The renowned Roberts, Oyster Rooms are to the left of the trailer car. Relaunched in 2015, the set is now still operational as part of the Heritage Fleet in attractive green and cream livery.

METROPOLE Brush-built single-deck railcoach 622, introduced in 1937, passes behind the Metropole Hotel on its way to the Pleasure Beach on 31 August. *Steptoe and Son Ride Again* is still on at the Princess Cinema. Peeping out from the left front side of No 622 is a Wolseley 1300 in front of which is parked a Sunbeam Stiletto, while passing them is a Morris 1100.

Right: **METROPOLE** On rain-slicked track, OMO car No 4 and Balloon double-decker 706 travel south past Springfield Road on 22 July. After suffering accident damage in 1980, 706 was restored to its original open-top condition for the tramway centenary in 1985, running as *Princess Alice*, though it is not currently operational. To the left of the tram are a Mk III Ford Cortina, a Skoda S100/S110 and the tail end of a Triumph Herald.

Left: **METROPOLE** In balmier weather, with a packed load of happy holidaymakers, first-built Boat car 600 drifts south past a Ford Corsair and a Hillman Imp Van towards the Tower at the start of the street-running section to North Pier on 24 July. The passengers smile for Ray Ruffell's camera…

METROPOLE ...and open Boat 600 nears the other end of the street-track section behind the part-scaffolded Butlin's Metropole Hotel on the same day. The prototype tram's side panels were lower than on the rest of the Boat fleet.

METROPOLE Illuminated trams didn't just work during the Lights: the frigate *HMS Blackpool*, car 736, is about to rejoin the promenade reserved track after the Metropole section on 27 July. The Princess is showing *The Day of the Jackal*.

METROPOLE Flanked by Morris Minor PKJ 864G, now-preserved Coronation 660 enters the street-running section at the Metropole behind two Balloon double-deckers on 3 August.

METROPOLE A Volkswagen Beetle emerges rather precariously from Springfield Road on 22 July between Coronation 662 and Balloon 722, both heading south past Butlin's Metropole Hotel.

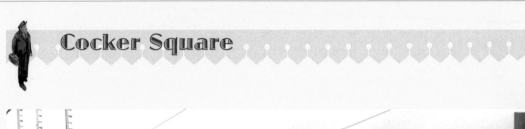

Cocker Square

COCKER SQUARE Cocker Square, named after one of the town's founding fathers, Dr William Cocker, was the northern terminus of the original 1885 conduit tramway – the first of its kind in the world. Coronation car 655 is bound for Starr Gate on 29 July. The imposing domed turret on the building at the corner is no longer there.

COCKER SQUARE
Revill's Hotel and the Regent Court flats form the backdrop on 25 July as Brush railcoach 635 works south to Manchester Square for the depot.

COCKER SQUARE A pair of double-deckers and a twin-car set near Cocker Square on 24 July. The multi-storey Regent Court flats, built in 1961, are on the right.

COCKER SQUARE Balloon double-decker 722 descends from Cocker Square towards North Pier on its journey to Starr Gate on 1 August. On the right parked are two cars of contrasting price brackets with a Humber Sceptre and in front (partially visible) the far lower priced Reliant Robin.

COCKER SQUARE Open Boat 605 works a well-patronised 'Circular' tour near Cocker Square on 25 July. The tram is now preserved in the United States. Parked to the left of the tram is an earlier version of the Humber Sceptre than that seen in the previous image; both were a product of the Rootes Group, by this time Chrysler (UK), part of the Chrysler Corporation of America. The various parts of Chrysler (UK) were by the end of 1978 sold to Peugeot and Renault.

1973 Happenings (3)

July
The British Library is established

Live and Let Die, starring Roger Moore as James Bond, is released

The Bahamas gain full independence from the UK

£20 million is paid to Thalidomide victims

Eighteen miners are killed when the brake mechanism on their cage fails at Markham Colliery, Derbyshire

The New York Dolls release their debut album

August
England goalkeeper Gordon Banks announces his retirement after losing the sight in one eye in a car crash

The coroner in the Bloody Sunday inquest accuses the Army of 'sheer unadulterated murder' after the jury returns an open verdict

More than 50 people die in a fire at the Summerland amusement centre in Douglas, Isle of Man

September
IRA bombs explode in Manchester and London's Victoria Station. Two days later, King's Cross and Euston Stations are bombed

The fashion store Biba reopens in London

Jackie Stewart becomes World Drivers' Champion after the Italian Grand Prix

Chile's democratic government is overthrown in a US-backed coup led by General Augusto Pinochet

October
LBC, Britain's first legal commercial independent radio station, broadcasts

Prime Minister Edward Heath announces plans for a price and pay code to fight inflation

The film *Don't Look Now* is released in a double bill with *The Wicker Man*

The Dalai Lama makes his first visit to Britain

Troops are drafted in to run fire stations in Glasgow after firefighters strike

The Yom Kippur War, the fourth and biggest Arab-Israeli conflict, is waged for nearly three weeks

Three Provisional IRA prisoners escape from Mountjoy jail by helicopter

COCKER SQUARE Working towards Uncle Tom's Cabin, Balloon car 711 passes a request stop on North Promenade on 1 August. The 1934-built tram has now been modified to form part of Blackpool Transport's 'B' fleet for use at busy times.

COCKER SQUARE Cream-coloured railcoach 638 is heading for Manchester Square and the depot in this view on 1 August. After an unsuccessful trial as an early OMO car, the tram was restored to two-person operation and later scrapped.

1973 Happenings (4)

November

The Second Cod War between Britain and Iceland ends

Miners begin an overtime ban

Last of the Summer Wine is first aired on BBC 2

Eight members of the Provisional IRA are convicted of the March bombings

Princess Anne marries Captain Mark Phillips at Westminster Abbey

December

The Sunningdale Agreement is signed by Edward Heath, Irish Premier Liam Cosgrave and Northern Ireland political parties

The motorway speed limit is temporarily cut to 50mph because of the Middle East oil crisis

As a result of coal shortages after industrial action, the Three-Day Week comes into force at midnight on 31 December

Gerald Ford is sworn in as US Vice-President

Spanish Premier Luis Carrero Blanco is assassinated by Basque separatist group ETA

The film *The Sting* is premiered in New York

COCKER SQUARE Progress twin-car set 676/686 passes Cocker Square on its journey to Bispham on 1 August. The tram is now preserved by the Blackpool Heritage Trust, though not operational. Ahead of it is the seemingly ubiquitous Balloon 715.

COCKER SQUARE Blackpool-based Empire Pools were another big advertiser on the town's trams. Balloon 701 is by Revill's Hotel near Cocker Square on 25 July. The jackpot can't compete with today's massive lottery payouts, even allowing for inflation.

COCKER SQUARE Open Boat 603, on a Coastal Tour, and Starr Gate-bound twin-car 679, operating singly without a trailer, pass the Stretton Hotel on North Promenade on 29 July. The car in front of No 603 is a two-door version of the Simca 1100.

COCKER SQUARE With Fleetwood showing on its destination blind, towing car 673 and its trailer 683 climb towards Cocker Square from the Metropole on 30 July. The driver is controlling the tram from the trailer cab as it is propelled by the power car. The driver of the Mk III Cortina travelling in the opposite direction has his window fully down indicating perhaps that this was a warm day in Blackpool.

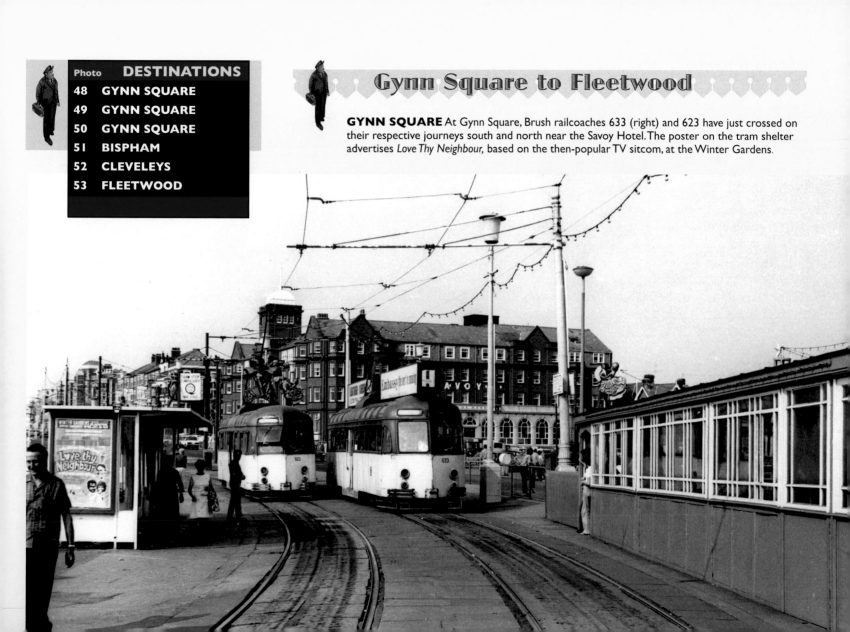

Gynn Square to Fleetwood

GYNN SQUARE At Gynn Square, Brush railcoaches 633 (right) and 623 have just crossed on their respective journeys south and north near the Savoy Hotel. The poster on the tram shelter advertises *Love Thy Neighbour,* based on the then-popular TV sitcom, at the Winter Gardens.

Right: **GYNN SQUARE**
Working without a trailer, twin-car 680 picks up passengers at Gynn Square on 1 August. The former towing railcoach, which now runs on loan as part of the Heritage Fleet, was one of the three twin-car motor vehicles that were not permanently coupled to a trailer, and became a 'solo' car permanently from 1972.

Right: **GYNN SQUARE**
The Savoy Hotel is in the background as Brush single-decker 627 tackles the short but demanding climb from Gynn Square to North Promenade on 1 August. Until 1963, trams would turn off to the right here for the trip along Dickson Road on the No 1 route to North Station.

BISPHAM At 11.15am on 27 July, open Boat car 600 has completed its journey to Bispham and will soon be reversed on the three-track layout that was used to handle short-working trams. Note the tank tops and flared trousers. From here, a single track led off down Red Bank Road to the original, six-road depot of the Blackpool and Fleetwood Tramroad, which closed in 1963 and is now the site of a Sainsbury's supermarket. The next station building on the way north is at Little Bispham, which is more of an Art Deco style than the neo-classical Bispham. The single-track turning circle at Little Bispham opened in 1938, a year after the double-track one at the Pleasure Beach.

1973 Departures

Lyndon B. Johnson	Ex-US President (b 1908)	22 January
Edward G. Robinson	Actor (b 1893)	26 January
Francis Romney	Cricketer (b 1873)	28 January
Harold Gibbons	Cricketer (b 1904)	16 February
Elizabeth Bowen	Novelist (b 1899)	22 February
Noel Coward	Composer and playwright (b 1899)	26 March
Pablo Picasso	Artist (b 1881)	8 April
A. C. Ewing	Philosopher (b 1899)	14 May
Jimmy Clitheroe	Comedian (b 1921)	6 June
Roger Delgado	Actor (b 1918)	18 June
Nancy Mitford	Novelist (b 1904)	30 June
Charles Ernest Garforth VC	Soldier (b 1891)	1 July
Betty Grable	Actor (b 1916)	2 July
John Brown Hamilton VC	Soldier (b 1896)	18 July
Bruce Lee	Martial arts expert (b 1940)	20 July
Cecil Griffiths	Olympic gold medallist (b 1901)	29 July
James Beck	Actor (b 1929)	6 August
J. R. R. Tolkien	Writer (b 1892)	2 September
W. H. Auden	Poet (b 1907)	29 September
Hilda Plowright	Actor (b 1890)	9 October
Pablo Casals	Cellist (b 1876)	22 October
Laurence Harvey	Actor (b 1928)	25 November
David Ben-Gurion	Ex-Israeli Prime Minister (b 1886)	1 December
Sir Robert Watson-Watt	Inventor (b 1892)	5 December
Henry Green	Novelist (b 1905)	13 December

CLEVELEYS The small but sedate resort of Cleveleys has always been a well-used intermediate stop on the tramway between Blackpool and Fleetwood. On 3 August, Balloon 711, English Electric railcoach 615 (converted to OMO car No 11 in 1975) and twin-car 677/687 wait at the stop, which is located near Victoria Road, right in the centre of the town.

Index of Blackpool tram types

Balloon Double-Decker: 1, 4, 5, 7, 9, 15, 16, 17, 19, 21, 27, 30, 31, 34, 35, 37, 39, 40, 47, 48

Boat Open Car: 5, 7, 11, 16, 17, 25, 27, 28, 36, 41, 45

Brush Railcoach: 12, 17, 24, 25, 26, 33, 38, 43, 44

Coronation Single-Decker: 18, 23, 24, 30, 31, 32

English Electric Railcoach: 47

Illuminated Car: 10, 29

OMO Car: 3, 6, 7, 9, 10, 11, 14, 17, 20, 27

Progress Towing Car: 41, 44

Progress Twin-Car: 8, 10, 13, 22, 24, 25, 34, 39, 42, 47

FLEETWOOD Fleetwood finale… Balloon double-decker 711 prepares for the 11-mile journey back to Starr Gate from the terminus at Fleetwood Ferry on 3 August. Despite successive threats to its existence, the little ferry still plies to the seaside settlement of Knott End on the other side of the Wyre estuary – an excellent example of integrated transport between tramway and waterway. Many readers will remeber the cars of the day with, amongst others, Ford represented by an Escort and the earlier Anglia. Rootes Group are 'sporting' a two-door Sunbeam Rapier, always considered that bit quicker than the Hillman variant, and a Vauxhall Viva is parked outside the ferry terminal. Austin are not to be left out of the picture, with a Maxi approaching in the distance.

Old STONEHAVEN

by

Brian H. Watt

STONEHAVEN SNAPSHOTS.

First published in the United Kingdom, 2000,
reprint 2005, 2007
by Stenlake Publishing Ltd.
Telephone: 01290 551122
www.stenlake.co.uk

ISBN 9781840330144

The publishers regret that they cannot supply
copies of any pictures featured in this book.

I would like to dedicate this book to my late father, ROBERT JOHN WATT.

ACKNOWLEDGEMENTS

The author would like to thank the various people who helped in the
preparation of, and research for, this book and in particular Elaine A. Collie.
The publishers would like to thank Robert Grieves for providing the picture that
appears on the front cover, Gordon Urquhart for providing the picture on the inside
back cover and W.A.C. Smith for providing the picture on the back cover

FURTHER READING

The books listed below were used by the author during his research. None of
them are available from Stenlake Publishing. Those interested in finding out
more are advised to contact their local bookshop or reference library.

Highways and Byways Round Stonehaven, Archibald Watt, 1984.
Picturesque Stonehaven, J. Reid, second edition 1906.
60 years at Stonehaven Outdoor Pool, 1994.
Stonehaven Golf Club Centennial Publication, 1988.
Stonehaven – Historical and Descriptive, W. Jolly and Sons, Albany Press, Aberdeen, 1897.
Stonehaven of Old Vol. 1, Stonehaven Heritage Society, 1989.
Stonehaven of Old Vol. 2, Stonehaven Heritage Society, 1995.
The Empty Shore – The Story of Cowie, Elizabeth Christie, 1980.
The Haven Under the Hill – The Story of Stonehaven, Elizabeth Christie, 1977.
Leopard Magazine 1979-1995.
Statistical Accounts of Scotland for Dunnottar and Fetteresso parishes.
Various Stonehaven official guidebooks from the 1970s and eighties.

INTRODUCTION

There are several conflicting views on the origins of the name Stonehaven, but the following derivation appears to fit the town appropriately: '*Stonehaven* – The Stanehive, Stanehyf, and Stanehiffe. *Stein*, stony, and *hyf*, or D. *haven*, port or shelter. The stony haven or bay, which is an exact description of (1) the strand between the Bellman's Heads and Downie, (2) the larger bay of Stonehaven.'

Stonehaven has a rich and varied history, with evidence of prehistoric activity in the area substantiated both by the standing stones and the Bronze Age, Iron Age and Pictish relics discovered in and around the town. Evidence also exists of a Roman presence in the area, with a Roman camp established near where Fetteresso Church now stands, and a much larger marching camp at Raedykes. As Stonehaven Bay was a natural harbour, it likely sheltered Roman galleys between their raids on the other small coastal settlements of the north-east.

The establishment of Stonehaven as a settlement can be traced to around the fifth century when a group of houses clustered round the inlet north of Downie Point, and the missionary St Ninian had a cell 160 feet above the sea at the rock of Dunnottar. The Parish Church of Dunnottar was consecrated on this rock in 1276 by William Wishart, Bishop of St Andrews.

Towards the end of the fourteenth century the rock of Dunnottar was owned by Sir William Keith, Marischal of Scotland, who constructed a castle on this consecrated ground. This resulted in his excommunication by the Bishop of St Andrews, a situation that was resolved only after Sir William built a new church, inland, for the people in 1397.

Until the beginning of the seventeenth century Stonehaven was an insignificant settlement existing in the shadow of Dunnottar Castle. Around 1600 the Earl Marischal was successful in persuading James VI to make Stonehaven the county town of Kincardine, taking over from Kincardine itself, two miles east of Fettercairn. In 1624 the town was elevated to a burgh of barony, with two bailies appointed to look after its affairs.

The next twenty-five years saw troubled times in Stonehaven, following the outbreak of civil war between King and parliament. A disagreement between the Earl Marischal (a Covenanter) and the Marquis of Montrose (a Royalist) led, in March 1645, to Montrose burning crops, farms, and houses in Dunnottar and Fetteresso parish – and even the boats in Stonehaven harbour.

A happier episode occurred in 1651 when the crown jewels of Scotland were sent to Dunnottar Castle, 'the strongest fortress in Scotland', to protect them from Cromwell's campaign. During Cromwell's eight-month siege of Dunnottar they were smuggled out, either by a fishwife in a creel, or by the wife of the minister of Kinneff and her maidservant in bundles of flax, depending on which version you favour! They were subsequently hidden beneath the pulpit of Kinneff Church until the Restoration.

In 1655 Thomas Tucker described Stonehaven as 'a little fisher town where goods have formerly been brought in, but not of late, because hindered from doing so by the neighbourhood and privileges of Montrose'. In 1656 Franck wrote: 'Now at the foot of this pavement [the old road from Aberdeen] there is a small harbour which they call Steenhive, but I take the liberty to call it stinking hive because it is so unsavoury; which serves only for pirates and picaroons [rogues]; but it bravely accommodates the Highlander for depredations [pillaging].' He goes on, however, to describe Dunnottar in very positive terms. Thereafter Stonehaven developed slowly, spreading back from the harbour and either side of High Street. Development was haphazard and living conditions were basic and harsh.

Stonehaven has fostered a diverse range of industries over the years, although fishing and agriculture have been dominant. Weaving was represented both by handloom weavers and mills making duck, canvas, and jute, as well as sailcloth, fishermen's stockings, sheeting linen, cotton wolsey, woollen blankets and other goods. The tanworks was a major employer producing boots, saddlery and latterly upholstery. Fishing encouraged coopering, boat-building, ropemaking and netmaking businesses. A lemonade factory, two breweries, two flour and meal mills and a distillery contributed to the 'well-being' of the inhabitants. Among the more unusual products of Stonehaven's manufacturing past are jew's harps, 'cutty' clay pipes and pipe lids.

The real development of the 'new town' of Stonehaven began when Robert Barclay of Ury purchased the lands of Arduthie, lying between the Carron and the Cowie, in 1759, reputedly for £1,500. Feus were made available and the River Carron was bridged (1781). The square (originally Barclay Square) was laid out, and streets planned in a gridiron pattern around it. Most of them were named after members of the Barclay family or their relatives, for instance: Gurney, Cameron, Ann, Margaret, David, Mary and Robert.

Prominent buildings and landmarks began to appear as the town expanded westwards: the Market Steeple in 1790; Dunnottar House, 1806; Fetteresso Parish Church, 1810; Market Buildings, 1826; the original Ramsay's shop, 1841. The railway opened in 1848; County Buildings (now the sheriff court and police station), 1863; the recreation grounds, 1885; the golf course, 1888; and the Bay Hotel, 1903.

From the 1890s until the present day Stonehaven has been a popular place of residence and holiday resort. The year 2000 sees the 400th anniversary of Stonehaven becoming the county town of Kincardine, and although it doesn't attract the numbers of holidaymakers it did in the early part of the century it remains a popular and thriving town, with much to offer both residents and visitors alike.

3

Castle St. Old Stonehaven.

Castle Street was originally the main road out of the old town to Dunnottar Castle. Note the fishing line drying on the spiltree (see page 9) and awaiting 'tipping' or cleaning. A wicker bow creel and pair of fisherman's boots are in the foreground, while two herring hakes, used for drying fish, can be seen on the wall in the background.

'The circus comes to town'. This print was made from a glass magic lantern slide, and is believed to date from the early 1890s. The big top has been erected on open ground next to the County Buildings (constructed 1863), which served as the county police headquarters from 1890 to 1949. At the top left of the picture is St Bridget's Mission Church, opened in January 1888 and designed by the architect John Young of Perth in Early English style.

HIGH STREET, STONEHAVEN.

51197.J.V.

High Street looking towards the market cross. The building in the left foreground with the ornamental pillars and crown lantern is known as Christian's House. It was constructed in 1712 and Episcopalian services were held there in the mid-eighteenth century, when repressive legislation prevented such gatherings. Cheekers Well, one of five wells serving the old town, can be seen further down the street on the right against the gable wall. The High Street is the venue for Stonehaven's famous fireball ceremony, which began in 1889 and has taken place on Hogmanay ever since (except during the war years). The swinging of tar- and rag-filled fireballs has its roots in a pagan rite to exorcise evil spirits.

6

The Inner Harbour packed with fishing boats around the turn of the century when the fishing industry – although still important in the life of the town – was beginning to go into decline. In the centre of picture is the Marine Hotel, built in 1886. The white building further to the right is the Ship Inn, dating from 1771. The building to the far right with two sets of doors is the lifeboat station which was closed down in 1934. Shortly after the last lifeboat was sold and removed.

The fleet leaving the harbour at the turn of the century on its way to the fishing grounds. The boats in the picture are mainly Zulus, which were first constructed around 1880 and so-called because they dated from the time of the Zulu war. They had a keel length of over 70 feet with a beam of around 25 feet and masts of up to 60 feet. Note the crowds seeing the fleet off and the herring barrels stacked at the pier ends.

At the Well, Stonehaven

Left: Two young girls enjoy a drink from the well at the end of the fish jetty. The well was recently refurbished as part of the Shorehead Environmental Improvements, and is in working order today. The girl standing by the well appears in several postcard views of Stonehaven and may have been the daughter of a local photographer.

Right: A Stonehaven worthy redding the fishing line. Redding was one of the men's tasks and required a spiltree to hold the spools of line like hanks of wool. One end of the spiltree was supported by a crosstree, and the other tied to a nearby post or supported on a dyke. The fisherman sat on a stool or chair to the right of his spiltree, uncoiling the line and feeding it into a wicker scull. At the same time he checked for (and repaired) any broken, frayed or missing snoods or hooks. In this case the spiltree is secured to the post which supported the leading light, used to guide ships into harbour.

An evocative photograph showing Shorehead around the turn of the century, and probably taken during the summer months as the men aren't wearing topcoats and the small boy is barefoot. The prominent four-storey building in the centre is now the Aberdeen and Stonehaven Yacht Club headquarters, while the large building in the distance was originally the granary. The fishing fleet is at sea, but herring barrels are lined up neatly on the Shorehead awaiting their return.

A group of fishermen 'having a news' around the turn of the century, probably discussing the day's catch. A84 was the *Sir George Balfour*, owned by James Christie in 1898. At 56 feet, she had the second greatest keel length of the thirty-seven boats fishing from Stonehaven at the time. The two-wheeled handcart in the background would have been used for moving gear around the harbour. Heavy mooring rings such as the one in the foreground are still in use around the harbour today.

This photograph was taken outside Nos. 13 and 14 Shorehead, adjacent to Wallace Wynd. When not engaged in collecting bait or preparing or baiting the lines, fisherwoman still had plenty to do, minding the baby and catching up on the latest news at the same time. Fish are drying on the herring hake attached to the wall, and a traditional shutter can be seen on the window in Wallace Wynd.

A fisherwoman on Shorehead baiting lines, closely watched by her granddaughter. The woman is wearing the traditional garb of a heavy woollen skirt topped by a close-fitting bodice shaped like a jacket. Baiting involved carefully removing the line from a wicker 'rusky' (out of sight on the woman's left) and coiling it carefully in the bottom of the scull on her right. Each hook was baited with a mussel or limpet as it passed between baskets, and the hooks were carefully laid on a cross-bit placed across the scull to prevent them tangling. It was a long and tiresome job!

Looking back to Shorehead from the middle pier, with the attractive reflections of Fifies and Zulus lying peacefully in harbour.

Local fishwives around the turn of the century, hard at work gutting and filleting the fish. This was cold, harsh and dirty work. The picture is full of the fishing paraphernalia of the time, from the herring hakes and waterproofs on the walls, to the creels and tubs and wooden-wheeled barrow, used to transport the lines and fish-boxes to and from the boats.

12

The Old Tolbooth, Stonehaven.

The Tolbooth (foreground) was built at the end of the sixteenth century by the 5th Earl Marischal as a storehouse for Dunnottar Castle. In 1600, when Stonehaven became the county town of Kincardine, it was adapted to serve as the sheriff courthouse and prison. It was converted to a store for local fishermen and merchants in 1767, and was subsequently used for the sale of fishing gear and ships chandlery. The building lay empty and deteriorated between the wars, suffering damage to its roof in November 1944 when a mine which drifted in on the tide exploded in the harbour. Having been restored it was reopened by the Queen Mother in 1963, and now serves as a museum and excellent seafood restaurant. The pedestal sundial at the top of the harbour steps dates from 1710.

Line-fishing in Stonehaven died out in the late 1940s and was succeeded by trawlers and seine netters which principally fished for cod, haddock and flatfish. Fishing fortunes in Stonehaven fluctuated, but this picture, taken on 8 October 1966, shows sufficient fish landed to warrant a sale on the quayside. The lorry in the background belongs to George Fraser, fish merchant.

Taken from the Bervie Braes, this picture looks over the old Invercarron tollhouse (foreground, now a private house) towards the Invercarron Dam, constructed to serve the now demolished Invercarron Mills. The dam was filled-in in 1970 and houses constructed on the site. Prominent in the centre, directly behind the dam, is the South Church. On the left is Jack's net factory which was established around 1860 in the High Street in the old town. The factory played its part in the First World War, manufacturing steel nets to ensnare submarines. The allotments on the right gradually made way for private houses in Victoria Street and Dunnottar Avenue, developed between 1900 and 1934.

Combination Poorhouse, Stonehaven

Of the nineteen parishes in the County of Kincardine, sixteen formed the Kincardineshire Poor Law Combination (Garvock, Nigg and St Cyrus opted out), and the poorhouse for these sixteen parishes was located in Stonehaven. It opened on 18 August 1867 with the admission of 'five ordinary poor'. A total of 116 'ordinary poor' were admitted in its first year of operation. Demands put on the poorhouse resulted in extensions and alterations being made in 1896, 1913 and 1928. From 1948 the building operated as Woodcot Hospital, a hospital for the care of the elderly, but this closed in 1998 and the former poorhouse is currently being converted into flats.

This photograph, probably taken in the 1860s, shows Stonehaven's meal mill. Pig-shaped weathervanes, such as the one in this picture, were a traditional feature of meal mills in the area. The mill later became an egg-packing station before being demolished and replaced by the present Mill Inn filling station. Prior to the coming of the railway in 1850 the Mill Inn (right) was an important stopping and refreshment point for stagecoaches travelling between Aberdeen, Montrose and Edinburgh. When this picture was taken it was a temperance hotel, but it operated as a licensed premises until 1997 when it was seriously damaged by fire. It was converted to private flats in 1998.

Looking north along Allardice Street around the turn of the century. The group of children are standing in front of the then Commercial Hotel (now the Queens Hotel), on the corner of Cameron Street. An advert for the hotel from a turn-of-the-century guidebook lists the various forms of transport available there, including landaus, waggonettes, brakes and 'dog carts', 'supplied on the shortest notice and on most moderate terms'. The large building on the right of this picture was William Mowat and Sons tannery, which in its heyday employed around 100 men. It was converted to flats in 1970.

Stonehaven's market buildings were commissioned by Captain Barclay-Allardice and built in 1826. The first part of the steeple – complete with clock and bell – was erected by public subscription in 1827. It was extended to its current height of 130 feet following further fund-raising in 1856. The right to hold a weekly market was granted by an Act of the Scots Parliament in 1663, and the square was the location for these markets, which were held on a Thursday. Sadly they no longer take place, but the square still hosts the annual feeing market on the first Saturday of June. This celebrates the feeing markets which traditionally took place twice a year, and at which local farm workers at the end of their 'term' congregated to be 'fee'd' to a new employer. Coaches such as the ones in this picture offered circular tours of the area. Note the old-style telephone box beside the pends.

210364 J.V.

Evan Street from the Square, Stonehaven.

Looking up a busy Evan Street from the Crown Hotel, with the attractive – and relatively car-free – Market Square on the right. One of Stonehaven's most famous residents, Robert William Thomson, was born 29 June 1822 in a house on the left of the picture overlooking the square. In 1845 Thomson invented the first pneumatic tyre, an invention normally credited to Dunlop who registered a patent some 43 years later. Mr Thomson also devised various other worthy inventions including a hydraulic floating dock, a portable steam crane and a fountain pen! His memory is celebrated in Stonehaven each year by the R. W. Thomson Memorial Vintage Vehicle Rally.

EVAN STREET, STONEHAVEN.

Looking down Evan Street towards Market Square from the corner of Ann Street in the early 1930s. The premises of David Waldie, printer, are about halfway down the street on the left. Waldie's was responsible for many of the fine photographic postcards prized by collectors today. The business continues to trade as a newsagent.

The north side of Market Square around the turn of the century. On the far left is the former Bank of Scotland, now the premises of the British Legion. The wall which protected the garden of the bank is the site of the current Bank of Scotland. The shops shown include Peter Christie, drapers; John Greig, jewellers and on the corner Taylors stationer and newsagent.

Charabancs lined up on the north side of Market Square waiting to transport visitors to the station, golf course or to Stonehaven's various visitor attractions. The original trees in the square were planted in 1856, although they have been replanted since then. The small fountain in the north-east corner of the square (visible at the front of the line of vehicles) was presented to the town council in 1897 by an Edinburgh lawyer and native of Stonehaven, Mr George Barrie. It is an attractive structure made of different types of granite from Aberdeen, Peterhead, Kemnay and Norway. A Bronze Age cist was found by workmen in this corner of the square in 1934. The Royal Hotel (background) was originally located in the upper floor of the market buildings.

MARKET SQUARE, STONEHAVEN.

The Queens Cinema in Allardice Street (now the site of Bruce Court) opened on Saturday 19 July 1913. The prospect of a cinema in Stonehaven didn't meet with the approval of some of the local dignitaries, as the following report from the *Stonehaven Journal* records: 'It is understood that there is prospect of yet another cinema theatre being erected in Stonehaven in the neighbourhood of the Auction Mart, some property having been purchased by an Aberdeen syndicate with, it is said, this object in view. While no doubt these shows will appeal to a certain class of visitors for whom the splendours of nature are insufficient in themselves and who crave for some sort of man made joy, yet it is not likely to lengthen the season here. Might we suggest that influence should be brought to bear on these gentlemen to alter their purpose and erect public baths instead. The situation would be very suitable for such a project.' Their pleas were made in vain!

AERIAL VIEW OF STONEHAVEN.

An interesting aerial view of the central part of Stonehaven taken in the early 1920s. The full extent of William Mowat's tannery buildings, extending either side of the lane known at the time as Tanneree Close (now Salmon Lane), can be seen in the left foreground. Market Square dominates the centre of the picture with Hugh Ramsey's shop (with awnings) at the top left. The River Cowie is in the foreground, flowing parallel to the back of the town prior to joining the Carron and entering the sea.

24

The semicircular roof of the Queens Cinema is visible in the centre foreground of this picture. One of Stonehaven's breweries stands on the far right at the corner of Barclay Street. Directly above it the majestic lines of Bath Street lead up to the Heugh Hotel, built at the turn of the century. Fetteresso Church, dating from 1810, is on the right just before the hotel. Prominent in the centre of the photograph is the five-storey Bay Hotel, built in 1903. The Cowie can again be seen flowing between the town and the beach, with access to the beach provided by three bridges. The bathing huts were segregated and one row was for men and the other for women!

The view from the bottom of Belmont Brae looking south along David Street and Barclay Street in the early 1900s. Just visible on the right of the picture are the buildings of one of Stonehaven's breweries (now the site of Kwikfit). Some of the brewery's vaults and the base of its chimney still exist under the Robert Burns memorial garden at the foot of Belmont Brae.

Gurney Street, one of the most elegant streets in Stonehaven. Many of these houses were let to visitors in the summer, 'with or without attendance' (i.e. with or without servants and other staff). Before they were built a small croft with two cows occupied the area. Because his croft was near the school, the crofter was often the target of local boys who taunted him with a verse quoted as:

Jonnie Kinnear, he milked the mear,
An Gollichie made the cheese,
His milks aye sour, his face's aye dour,
An' his butters' aye covered wi' flees!

St.Leonards Red Cross Hospital, Stonehaven.

81345. J.V.

This building was originally a family home for James Jack, a prominent and wealthy fish merchant in Stonehaven and owner of Jack's net factory at Invercarron. During the First World War it was converted for use as a military hospital and the walls of the wards were reputedly painted red, white and blue. The building subsequently became a private house again, but is now a popular hotel enjoying spectacular views over Stonehaven Bay.

CAMPING GROUND AND ENTRANCE TO RECREATION
GROUNDS, STONEHAVEN.

A2842.

This 1950s picture shows the former camping ground adjacent to the River Cowie at Cowie Bridge. The old mill lade, which served the Cowie Mills, can be seen between the tents and the roadway. The camping ground has now been moved to the caravan park at Cowie and this area is used as a quoiting ground by Dunnottar Quoiting Club, formed in 1890. In the background are the recreation grounds which were opened in 1885 with bowling, tennis and putting facilities, provided for the increasing number of visitors to the town.

28

STONEHAVEN.
WALDIE, 9 H. EVAN ST.

Stonehaven beach in the early 1920s illustrating its popularity for bathing. The motor launch in the background ran trips from the beach to Fowlsheugh bird sanctuary or Dunnottar Castle. A crowd is waiting at the landing stage on the beach for the next trip. The prominent building on the left was known as the 'Red Shelter' and had an upper balcony which was a popular vantage point for viewing the beach. The shelter survived many fierce winter storms but was demolished just after the Second World War, shortly before the present beach promenade was constructed.

29

ON THE BEACH, STONEHAVEN.

1495

Stonehaven beach in the early 1900s looking back towards the centre of town. The Red Shelter and boardwalk are visible on the right of the picture, with the two sets of bathing huts (men's and women's) in the background. The rowing boats drawn up on the beach belonged to Sandy Clark the boatbuilder, and were available for hire.

An early 1900s photograph taken from the upper balcony of the Red Shelter, looking along the promenade path towards the town. The path had to be relaid every summer because of the damage caused by winter storms. Judging by the crowds, this picture was taken in July when the number of visitors from Glasgow and Aberdeen was greatest. The large wheels which can be seen in the background at the waterline supported the landing stage for motor launch trips. The stage was also used by children as a diving platform.

31

Stonehaven beach receiving the full force of a 'sou-easter'. Spectacular storms such as this caused much damage to the beach, boardwalks and buildings, and the Red Shelter, prominent in the middle of the picture, was destroyed by such a storm after the Second World War. Such storms often attracted large crowds to the beach, many risking life and limb for the best view.

A "SOUTH EASTER" AT STONEHAVEN BEACH, A. ROSS.

This early 1900s picture was taken at the point where the Cowie now enters the sea and looks south along the river's original course between the town and the beach. The bridge in the view was known as Sivies Brig and was the most northerly of the three bridges between the town and beach. The chimneys in the background were part of the tannery buildings.

TREES JAMMED BY SPATE
AT BRIDGE OF COWIE,
STONEHAVEN.

Labourers attempting to clear logs jammed against Cowie Bridge, brought down from the woods to the west of Stonehaven by a serious spate (believed to be in the 1930s). The bowling greens, in the background, are still submerged by floodwater. A few years later work was undertaken to strengthen the banks of the river at this point to prevent the regular flooding of the recreation grounds by the Cowie in times of spate.

Looking across the recreation grounds from the esplanade in the early 1900s, with tennis courts on what is now the site of the putting green. The grounds were opened in 1885 and were considered to be a 'great attraction to the Town'. At the turn of the century a four-person family season ticket for the tennis courts cost £1; promenade tickets giving right of admission to the grounds but no right to play were issued at 5 shillings for a family of four. Prominent in the background is the Bay Hotel, built in 1903 by a group of local businessmen. The 40-bedroomed hotel quickly became Stonehaven's foremost place to stay, and was described as one of the outstanding hotels of the north-east by virtue of 'its commanding situation overlooking the Bay . . . its reputation founded on courtesy and a service that embraces a liberal table and well stocked wine cellar'. In 1970 the hotel was converted to a Church of Scotland Eventide Home.

STONEHAVEN FROM THE BEACH   A. ROSS.

The bowling green and recreation ground pavilion have changed little since this photograph was taken just after the First World War. The pavilion was the clubhouse for the Thistle Cricket Club when their pitch was located within the grounds of Cowie House.

STONEHAVEN SWIMMING POOL

Stonehaven's outdoor swimming pool was opened on 2 June 1934 and 2,300 people turned out for the event. However, the pool was only built after a poll of the town's residents decided 656 to 539 in favour of construction going ahead. The project cost £9,529. This 1934 picture shows one of the popular weekly galas which included log rolling, bathtub races and diving displays from the 6-metre diving board, as well as swimming competitions. A heating system was added before the 1935 season raising the water temperature to 58F, which greatly increased visitor numbers (the water temperature is now maintained as close to 85F as possible, the same as the indoor pool!). Apart from disruptions during the war years, the pool remained popular up until the 1960s. From the sixties onwards its fortunes were mixed, with plant and maintenance problems and declining visitor numbers. The pool was threatened with closure in recent years but has received a new lease of life due to the dedication of a community group who have taken over the running of what is one of Stonehaven's finest assets.

This aerial view illustrates Dunnottar Castle's inaccessible location, the feature that made it readily defensible. Few Scottish castles have witnessed as many important historical events as Dunnottar, and although these are well-documented elsewhere, certain episodes deserve a brief mention. The castle was stormed in 1297 by Sir William Wallace, who burned the English garrison alive in the church where they had taken sanctuary. What was perhaps Dunnottar's finest hour came in the year 1651 when, having been besieged by Cromwell's troops for eight months, the Honours of Scotland (comprising crown, sword and sceptre) were smuggled out and hidden in old Kinneff Church. The castle's blackest moment was in 1685 when 167 Covenanters were imprisoned in the Whig's Vault, many of them dying through ill-treatment or torture. Dunnottar was sold to the York Building Company in 1720 and subsequently partially dismantled. It was not restored or repaired until 1925 when it was purchased by the late Viscountess Cowdray. In 1990 Dunnottar was used in the filming of Franco Zefferelli's *Hamlet*, starring Mel Gibson.

Dunnottar Castle has seen many visits by the monarchy, and this picture relates to a surprise visit reported in the *Stonehaven Journal* of 29 September 1910: 'On Saturday the Queen and Princess Mary, accompanied by Lady Mary Grefusis, Lord Rosebery, the Marquis de Soverd, Portuguese Ambassador, and Sir Henry Legge paid a visit to Dunnottar Castle. The royal party left Balmoral in two motors and drove by way of Banchory and the Slug Road to Stonehaven. Reaching the town a brief halt was made and one or two places visited, after which the journey to the castle was resumed. On arriving at the gate, tickets were purchased from the custodian and the royal party were shown round the ruins and seemed to be deeply interested in the history of the buildings. Added to the fine weather the Royal Party had the advantage of almost privacy, the only other visitors being 2 Japanese gentlemen, who arriving at the room where the visitors book is left, at about the same time as the Royal Party, remained in the background till the party from Balmoral had signed the visitors book, the signature of the Queen being simply the word "Mary". It is now 260 years since the Castle was last visited by a Sovereign, King Charles I visiting it on 8th July 1650. Previous to that was King James IV on 15th October 1504 and King James VI on 18th June 1580, so that in a period of 406 years it has been visited by four of the reigning houses, 3 of whom must have been struck by its strategic importance and its bustling activity.' The postcard is captioned 'Entrance to Dunnottar Castle, Stonehaven, & the keeper who conducted Queen Mary and party on the occasion of her surprise visit, 24th September 1910'. The picture may, however, not be all that it seems, as rumours at the time suggested that it was not in fact the keeper who attended to the royal visitors, but his wife as per usual!

Left: Most of the trees of Dunnottar Woods were planted in the early 1800s, and a century later there was established woodland over much of this area. Walking in the vicinity was a popular pastime for locals and visitors alike, and guides to Stonehaven from the beginning of the twentieth century refer to 'the fine trees in the wood and the squirrels which also abound'. Many of the original trees were felled shortly after the Second World War, and even more were lost in the Great Gale of 1953. Shortly afterwards the woods were purchased by the Forestry Commission and major replanting was undertaken. Dunnottar Woods are still owned by Forest Enterprise but a community group (the Dunnottar Woodland Park Association) now have a say in the management of what is today called the Dunnottar Woodland Park. The two organisations are jointly undertaking a range of works to further improve what is one of Stonehaven's most attractive assets.

Right: The Periwinkle Den is a small gorge within Dunnottar Woods, where the Glasslaw Burn descends some 200 metres through the local pudding-stone rock via a series of small torrents and waterfalls. The den gets its name from the abundance of lesser periwinkle (*vinca minor*) which carpeted the area at the turn of the century. The gentleman in the photograph is believed to be J. Watson, the person who took the photograph. Mr Watson had photographic premises in both Stonehaven and Inverbervie. The picture also shows the rustic wooden footbridge over the den which existed at the turn of the century. It is not clear when this bridge fell into disrepair but until recently all that remained were the stone buttresses at either end. The Dunnottar Woodland Park Association have recently installed a most attractive bridge in the same location.

The estate of Dunnottar belonged to the Keith family until 1782 when a portion was sold to Alexander Allardice. Dunnottar House was constructed in 1806, reputedly at a cost of £10,000, a considerable sum at that time. The expense was probably due in part to the extensive outbuildings, such as the large walled garden and stable block that were also built, as well as the extensive planting and landscaping undertaken. Eleanor Allardice (daughter of Alexander) married Lord William Kennedy in 1814 and took up residence in Dunnottar House. The property changed hands in 1835 and 1851, and in 1901 was purchased by Captain William Ritchie, owner of the town's Glenury Distillery. After his death it was let to various tenants but deteriorated steadily and was finally demolished in the late 1950s. No trace of the building remains today.

This rocky pool on the River Carron lies behind the north-east corner of Dunnottar Kirkyard. It is known locally as the Witches Pot (or Pool) or Deil's (Devil's) Kettle, and is reputedly where local witches were executed by 'ducking' or drowning. The practice was not abandoned very long ago, and the last witch to be executed in Scotland was killed as recently as 1722. Close by lies the Gallows Hill, the site of the old Stonehaven gallows, which from c.1600 was the execution site for convicted local criminals. The Witches Pot may also have served another role around this time, when the sentence for serious crimes was that 'men were hung and women were drowned'.

The Witches' Pot, Stonehaven

Cols memorating Peace Planting an Oak Tree behind Dunnottar Church

This picture depicts one of the events which took place on Saturday 8 July 1919, the day of Stonehaven's peace celebrations. An oak tree was planted in honour of parishioners who fought in the First World War on a piece of rough grazing in the glebe near the east wall of Dunnottar Cemetery. The tree, known locally as the Peace Tree, still stands and is now of considerable size. A granite plaque in the kirkyard wall nearby reads: 'This tree was planted 8th July 1919 in honour of those parishioners who fought in the Great War'. The town's peace celebrations included a flag day, the beach entertainers performing in the square, a picnic for some 2,000 children at Urie and a motor boat regatta in Stonehaven Bay.

Mineral Well, Urie Glen, Stonehaven

This mineral well, constructed from Peterhead granite in 1860, is located under the railway viaduct in the Mineralwell Park. Water was piped to it from an iron-rich spring which issued from Fetteresso Glebe and the well was renowned for its health-giving properties. It stands on the site of the holy well of St Kieran (properly St Caran) the patron saint of Fetteresso Parish, and the inscription on it reads: 'St Kierans Well erected by public subscription AD 1860'. As well as funds donated by the public, money for the well, along with the nearby cottage and road, was donated by the railway company. Such was the popularity of the chalybeate well that the gentlemen of Stonehaven 'considered each morning lost that did not see them early afoot to imbibe copious cooling draughts of 'ironeerie water' '. The well was restored by the community council in 1982 but sadly the water supply has since been severed and it again lies dry and overgrown.

The railway viaduct was constructed *c.*1848 to carry the Caledonian Railway line over the River Cowie and north towards Aberdeen from Stonehaven (there is an Aberdeen-bound train on the viaduct in the picture). Work to replace the original wooden arches with wrought iron began in 1882 and was completed in 1885. The viaduct is 1,100 feet long, over 100 feet high and built on a strong curve. The Mineralwell Croft can be seen nestling beneath it with its corn stacks drying in the field. This whole area was laid out as the Mineralwell Park in 1970 and the old croft buildings were demolished in 1981. Just out shot on the right lies the now derelict Glenury Royal Distillery, founded in 1824 by Captain Robert Barclay-Allardice on the site of an old flax mill on the banks of the River Cowie. The distillery was established to use excess barley following a slump in the market after the Peninsular War.

Whale Caught in Stonehaven Bay, 28th April, 1906

Despite the title of this postcard, it appears from newspaper reports of the time that this whale may have beached itself rather than been 'caught' by local fishermen. What is clear, however, is that it caused considerable local interest, and the *Stonehaven Journal* of 3 May 1906 reported: 'The fine weather and the attraction of a stranded whale at Crawton somewhat affected the attendance at Churches and Sunday Schools this week. The crowd on Sunday 29th April was very large. One gentleman on returning counted within a space of 2 miles as many as 550 persons going out to see the whale'. There is no record of the method of disposal of the whale's body!

The ruins of Cowie Kirk – or the Chapel of St Mary and St Nathalan to give it its correct name – lie in the foreground of this picture. The church was consecrated in 1276 by Bishop William Wishart of St Andrews, and was unroofed shortly before the Reformation, 'on account of scandals'. An old local verse claims: 'Between the kirk and the kirk ford, there lies St Nathalan's hoard'. No such treasure has yet been unearthed, perhaps because local people have not searched too diligently, being put off by the rumours of horrific and fatal consequences for the finder! Stonehaven Golf Club's 'new' clubhouse – opened on Wednesday 7 July 1897, with a further extension in 1899 to provide 'better accommodation for the ladies' – is in the background. The centenary publication produced by the club notes that one interesting feature of the new clubhouse was 'a liquor press for which each member was provided with a key and was (on trust) to honour the charges of 4d for a bottle of beer, 4d for a whiskey and 2d for a bottle of soda'. Clearly this facility proved an attraction to various non-members and the local press reported a number of break-ins in the following years. The current clubhouse is formed from additions and modifications to this original building.

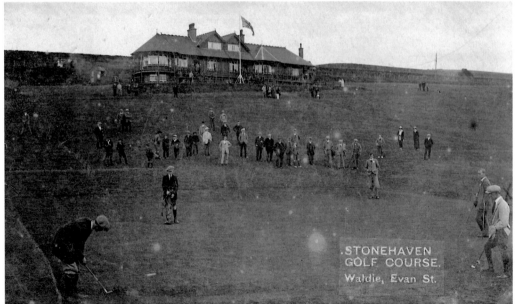

Stonehaven's original nine-hole golf course was laid out in the late 1880s or early nineties. In 1897 it was replaced by another 9-hole course spread over an extended area. The 18-hole course was opened in 1904 and laid out to the plans of Archie Simpson, the professional at the Royal Aberdeen Golf Club. This picture shows a competition or exhibition match on the 18th green, which judging by the number of spectators was of some significance. Regrettably the specific occasion or date is not recorded by the writer of the postcard, who only identifies himself as the player on the right wearing the cap.

A superb picture of four generations (and dog) of a local family around the turn of the century. The photograph was taken by Alex Ross, photo artist of Stonehaven, and shows examples of the fashions at the beginning of the twentieth century. Does anyone recognise their relatives?

STATION HOTEL, STONEHAVEN.

TEL. No. 57.

The Station Hotel was built following the arrival of the railway in Stonehaven in the late 1840s. It was originally known as Melvins Hotel and in the early days of the railway, before proper platforms, a bell rang in the hotel when trains were coming. The construction of the hotel caused much concern among hoteliers in the town centre who felt that their trade would suffer. However, the volume of visitors meant that their fears were unfounded, and it was the Station Hotel whose trade was affected in the 1920s when buses came into regular use and travellers turned once again to the roads. The Station Hotel is still in use and is a popular and well-patronised hotel.